DECORATIVE ARTS
In The J. Paul Getty Museum

Gillian Wilson

The J. Paul Getty Museum

L.C. 77-85357
ISBN 0-89236-007-0
Cover: Detail of no. 126

This book was designed in Los Angeles by Lilli Cristin. All text was set in Baskerville by R S Typographics. 5000 copies were lithographed on Warren's Lustro Dull paper by Graphic Press.

Photography credits: Edward Cornachio, nos. 2, 76, 96, 105; French & Co., no. 109; Joseph Klimna, Jr., nos. 61, 83, 101; Armando Solis, nos. 43, 50, 68, 70, 72, 89, 112; Taylor & Dull, nos. 13, 26, 36; Nemo Warr, no. 56. All other photography by Donald A. Hull.

INTRODUCTION

This book illustrates, in chronological order, nearly all the objects in the collection of decorative arts in the J. Paul Getty Museum. Only a few pieces of dubious date or inferior quality have been omitted. The objects, with the exception of some oriental or German ceramics and a pair of German commodes, were all made in France, and probably without exception in Paris.

The collection ranges in date from the 1660's to the 1790's. Of early nineteenth-century date is a chandelier, a set of seat furniture, an inkstand, and a secretaire. The book shows the extent of the collection up to the year 1977. A *catalogue raisonné* is being written, but it is not expected to be published for some years. Here, fairly detailed captions are provided for each object.

Gillian Wilson,
Curator of Decorative Arts

LIST OF CRAFTSMEN REPRESENTED IN THE COLLECTION
(Some of the names listed are given as attributions only)

Joseph Baumhauer, no. 65
Alexandre-Louis Bellangé, no. 135
Charles Buteux, no. 79
Louis-Simon Boizot, no. 128
Jean Boucault, no. 92
François Boucher, nos. 59, 76, 109
André-Charles Boulle, nos. 1, 15, 17, 18, 20
Jacques Caffieri, no. 52
Martin Carlin, nos. 96, 97, 98, 100
Jean-Baptiste Cheret, no. 90
Clodion, no. 120
Charles-Michel Cochois, no. 15
Charles Cressent, nos. 25, 38, 39, 50, 61
François de Cuvilliés, no. 48
Claude-Gabriel Dardet, no. 27
Adrien-Faizelot Delorme, no. 70, 81
Jean-Jacques Dieux, no. 131
Dodin, nos. 80, 86, 88
E. Doirat, no. 33
J.-F. Dominicé, no. 28
Jacques Dubois, nos. 73, 75
René Dubois, no. 101
L.-F. Feuchères, no. 116
Jean-Jacques Fieffé, no. 40
Nicolas-Alexandre Folin, no. 129
Alexandre Fortier, no. 51
Antoine Foullet, no. 85
Antoine Gaudreau, no. 22
François-Thomas Germain, no. 56
Jean-Joseph de Saint Germain, no. 61
Pierre Gouthière, nos. 103, 112, 113, 114, 115, 119
Jacques Gudin, no. 17
Georges Jacob, nos. 108, 125
Jacob Desmalter et Cie, no. 132
Pierre *le jeune,* no. 100
Gilles Joubert, no. 95
Roger Vandercruse La Croix, no. 91
Lapina, no. 85
Jean-Pierre Latz, nos. 51, 62
Jean-François Leleu, no. 82
Louis-Noël Malle, no. 93
Etienne Martincourt, no. 111
G. Merlet, no. 129
Bernard Molitor, no. 121
Philippe-Claude Montigny, no. 127
Morin, no. 89
Etienne le Noir, no. 67
Robert Osmond, no. 67
Jean-François Oeben, nos. 62, 68, 69, 83, 84
Nicolas Petit, no. 70
Jean-Henri Riesener, nos. 106, 120
Bernard van Risenburgh, nos. 41, 43, 44, 46, 54, 63, 72, 88
David Roentgen, no. 119
Jean Romilly, no. 61
Charles le Roy, no. 94
Julien le Roy, nos. 18, 52
Claude-Charles Saunier, no. 105
Jean-Baptiste-Claude Sené, no. 126
Jean-Baptiste Tandart, no. 105
Henri-François Vincent *le jeune,* no. 117
Adam Weisweiler, nos. 117, 118, 122

1
CABINET
French; c. 1670.
Veneered with marquetry of stained and natural woods, tortoise-shell, ebony, pewter, brass, ivory, and set with gilt-bronze mounts. The figures are of wood, painted to resemble patinated and gilded bronze. Behind the central door is an architectural fitting of pillars and niches, veneered with tortoiseshell, ebony and mirror glass, decorated with gilt-bronze. The name of the cabinet-maker is not known, but the piece is attributed to the royal cabinet-maker, André-Charles Boulle (1642–1732). It is likely that the cabinet was made for Louis XIV.
H. 89 in., (226.7 cm.), W. 53 in., (134.6 cm.)
76.DA.45

2
CARPET
French (Savonnerie); c. 1665.
The carpet is listed in the inventory of Louis XIV. It has been cut in length at some time, and the short borders are nineteenth-century replacements.
L. 263 in., (668.1 cm.),
W. 173 in., (439.5 cm.)
70.DC.63

3
TABLE
French (Gobelins?);
c. 1680–1690.
The table is veneered with tortoiseshell, pewter, brass, ebony, stained woods, and ivory. It was probably made in the royal workshops at the Gobelins. A number of very similar tables are described in the inventories of Louis XIV.
H. 28½ in., (72.4 cm.),
W. 44½ in., (112.4 cm.),
D. 30½ in., (77.5 cm.).
71.DA.100

4
SILK PANELS
French; c. 1680.
Of silk, woven with silver threads.
H. 21 in., (53.3 cm.), 31 in., (78.8 cm.).
76.DH.21

5
PAIR OF CANDLESTICKS
French; c. 1700.
Of gilt-bronze.
The shafts and bases are decorated with figures of children playing musical instruments.
H. 10 in., (25.4 cm.), Diam. 5¾ in., (14.6 cm.).
72.DF.56

6
MODEL FOR A CLOCK
French; c. 1700.
The model is made of terra cotta and was probably executed for a royal patron such as Louis XIV.
H. 31 in., (78.7 cm.),
W. 20½ in., (52.1 cm.),
D. 9½ in., (24.1 cm.).
72.DB.52

7
COMMODE
French; c. 1710.
The commode is veneered with *satiné rouge* and decorated with gilt-bronze mounts. It is branded on the back with the stamp of the Comte d'Artois and an "M" surmounted by an open crown, probably for the Château of Maisons-Laffitte.
H. 33¼ in., (84.4 cm.),
W. 55 in., (139.7 cm.),
D. 23¾ in., (60.3 cm.).
J.P.G.D.37

8
COMMODE
French; c. 1710.
Veneered with rosewood and decorated with gilt-bronze mounts. This commode by tradition is reputed to have been made for the Dauphin, and to have once stood in the Château of Meudon. However, there is no documentary evidence to substantiate this claim.
H. 33⅛ in., (84.1 cm.),
W. 48⅜ in., (122.9 cm.),
D. 22½ in., (57.2 cm.).
73.DA.66

9
PAIR OF BRONZE GROUPS
French; c. 1710.
The bronzes represent Boreas and Orithyia (left) and Pluto and Persephone (right). They are reductions of the marbles made by Gaspard Marsy (1624–1681) and Anselme Flamen (1647–1717) (Boreas), and François Giradon (1628–1715) (Pluto). The marble statues were made for the gardens of Versailles and were carved between the years 1680 and 1687.
Boreas: H. 21½ in., (54.6 cm.),
W. (at base) 8½ in., (21.6 cm.),
D. (at base) 8½ in., (21.6 cm.).
Pluto: H. 20¼ in., (51.4 cm.),
W. (at base) 8½ in., (21.6 cm.),
D. (at base) 8½ in., (21.6 cm.).
74.PB.18, 17

10
PAIR OF LIDDED VASES
The ceramic: Chinese (K'ang Hsi period) *famille verte*; 1662–1722.
The gilt-bronze mounts: French: c. 1710. H.16 in., (40.6 cm.), Diam. 11½ in., (29.2 cm.).
72.DE.50

11
WALL CLOCK
French; c. 1710.
Made of gilt-bronze, set with panels of blue painted shell. The nineteenth-century movement is an English replacement. It once housed a repeating movement, with strings to be pulled in the dark to release the repeating mechanism.
H. 27¼ in., (69.2 cm.),
W. 11¼ in., (28.6 cm.), D. 5 in., (12.7 cm.).
73.DB.74

12
CHANDELIER
French; c. 1710.
The frame is of silvered bronze, overlaid with glass. The drops are of glass, colored glass, and rock crystal.
H. 29½ in., (75 cm.), W. 32 in., (81.3 cm.).
74.DH.29

13
BRONZE
French; c. 1710.
The bronze, known as the Venus Marina, is stylistically comparable to the work of Robert le Lorrain (1666–1743). This bronze is sometimes used as part of a mantel clock.
H. 25½ in., (64.8 cm.),
W. (at base) 9½ in., (24.1 cm.),
D. (at base) 14½ in., (36.8 cm.).
74.PB.16

14
PAIR OF LIDDED VASES
The ceramic: Chinese (early K'ang Hsi period); c. 1650.
The gilt-bronze mounts: French; c. 1720.
H. 13½ in., (34.5 cm.),
W. 12¾ in., (32.4 cm.),
D. 13 in., (33 cm.).
75.DE.5

15
COMMODE
French; c. 1710.
The commode is veneered with tulipwood and amaranth, and is stamped "C. M. COCHOIS" for Charles-Michel Cochois (d. 1764). It is likely that Cochois merely restored this piece in the 1740's, and that it was made earlier in the workshops of André-Charles Boulle (1642–1732).
H. 34½ in., (87.6 cm.),
W. 50½ in., (128.3 cm.),
D. 23 in., (58.4 cm.).
70.DA.80

16
INKSTAND AND PAPERWEIGHTS
French; c. 1715.
Of gilt-bronze. Inkstands of identical model appear in two French portrait paintings. One, by Vigée Le Brun of Charles-Alexander de Calonne, was painted in 1784. The other portrait, by J. A. Aved of Jean-Gabriel de la Porte du Theil, was painted in about 1738.
Inkstand: H. 4⅛ in., (10.5 cm.), W. 14⅞ in., (37.8 cm.), D. 11⅛ in., (28.3 cm.).
Paperweight: H. 2⅝ in., (6.7 cm.), W. 4⅝ in., (11.8 cm.), D. 6½ in., (16.5 cm.).
75.DF.6

17
MANTEL CLOCK
French; c. 1715–1725.
The clock is veneered with ebony, brass, and tortoiseshell, decorated with gilt-bronze mounts. It was probably made in the workshops of André-Charles Boulle (1642–1732). A drawing for it, attributed to Boulle, is in the Musée des Arts Décoratifs, Paris. The movement is by Jacques Gudin (1706–1744).
H. 39¾ in., (101 cm.), W. 19 in., (48.4 cm.), D. 11½ in., (29.2 cm.).
72.DB.55

18
PEDESTAL CLOCK
French; c. 1710–1725.
Veneered with tortoiseshell and decorated with gilt-bronze mounts. The figures at the corners of the clock represent the four Continents known at that time. The movement is by Julien le Roy (1686–1759), and the case is attributed to André-Charles Boulle (1642–1732).
H. 131⅜ in., (335 cm.), W. 27⅜ in., (69.6 cm.), D. 14 in., (35.5 cm.).
74.DB.1

19
PAIR OF TORCHERES
French; c. 1725.
Of gilded wood.
H. 68¼ in., (173.3 cm.), Diam. 23 in., (58.4 cm.).
71.DA.98
(Candelabra: see cat. no. 31)

20
CHANDELIER
French; c. 1710.
Of gilt-bronze. The design is attributed to André-Charles Boulle (1642–1732).
H. 30½ in., (77.5 cm.),
W. 32 in., (81.3 cm.).
76.DF.13

21
CONSOLE TABLE
French; c. 1725.
Of gilded oak, with a marble top. The coat-of-arms centering the front would appear to be that of Colbert's second son, the Comte de Blainville.
H. 35¼ in., (89.5 cm.),
W. 60¼ in., (153 cm.),
D. 23½ in., (59.7 cm.).
72.DA.68

22
BIBLIOTHEQUE
French; c. 1725.
Veneered with king wood, decorated with gilt-bronze mounts. It is attributed to Antoine Gaudreau (1680–1751).
H. 102 in., (259.1 cm.),
W. 65 in., (165.1 cm.),
D. 16 in., (40.6 cm.).
74.DA.14

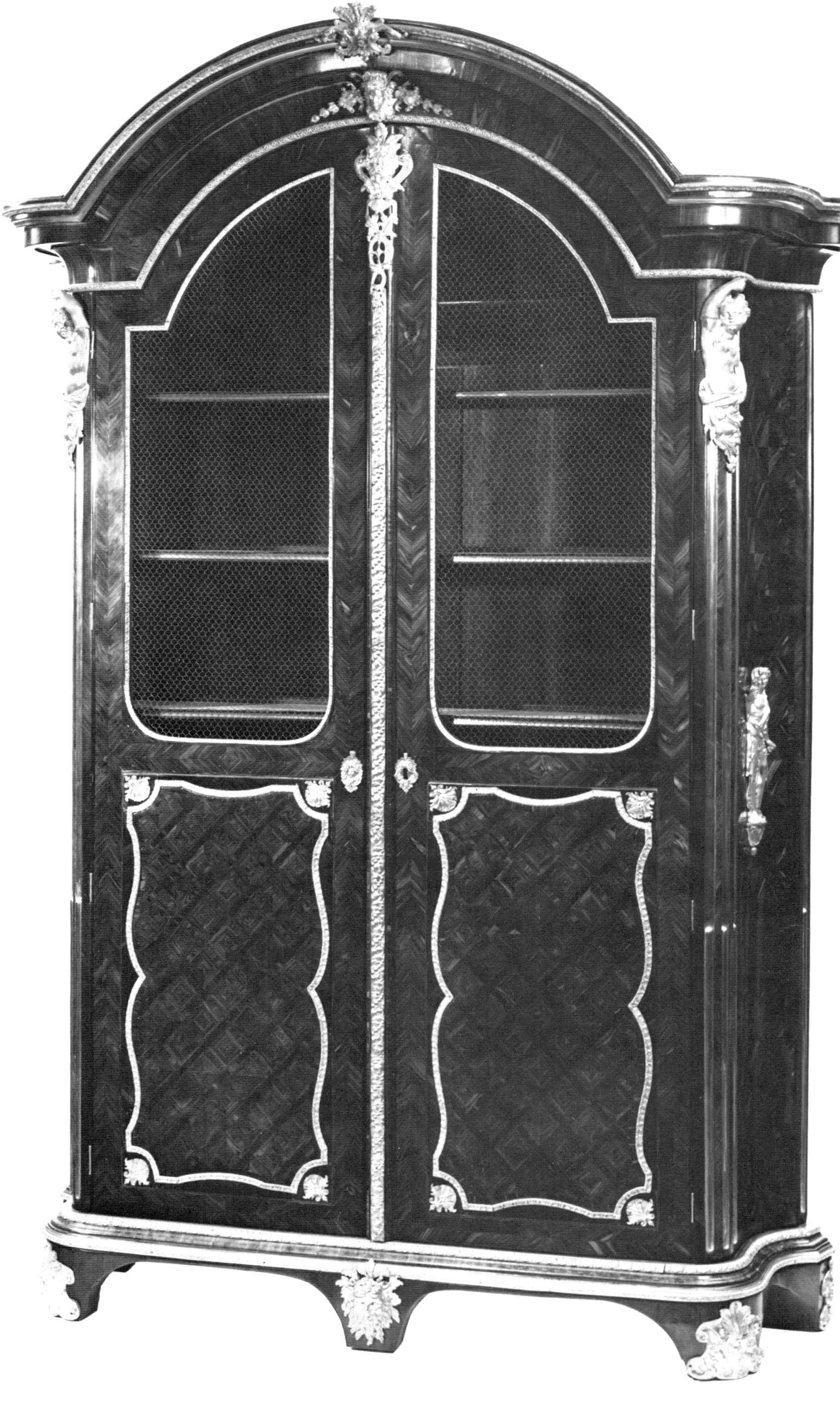

23
GARNITURE OF
FIVE VASES
Chinese (K'ang Hsi period); 1662–1722.
Jars: H. 12½ in., (31.8 cm.), Diam. 10¾ in., (27.3 cm.).
Beakers: H. 11⅛ in., (28.3 cm.), Diam. 5 in., (12.7 cm.).
72.DE.72

24
CARD TABLE
French; c: 1725.
Veneered with *satiné rouge*. It is a combined card table and writing table. When opened, the table top has a velvet surface for playing cards, dished borders to keep chips, and areas at each corner for cards. A section which can be pulled out at the back is fitted with a velvet writing surface and contains two drawers, one having an ink pot, sand pot, and a sponge box.
H. 30 in., (76.2 cm.), W. 40 in. (101.6 cm.), D. 30 in., (76.2 cm.).
75.DA.2

25
WRITING DESK *(Bureau plat)*
French; c. 1725.
Veneered with *satiné rouge* and amaranth, decorated with gilt-bronze mounts. The table is attributed to Charles Cressent (1685–1768). An identical table appears in a full length portrait of Said Pasha, ambassador from Constantinople, painted by J. A. Aved in 1742. The painting is at the Château of Versailles.
H. 29 in., (73.7 cm.), W. 79 in., (200.7 cm.), D. 35 in., (89 cm.).
67.DA.10

26
LIDDED BOWL
The ceramic: Japanese (Imari); c. 1680.
The silver mounts: French; 1722–1727.
H. 8½ in., (21.6 cm.),
W. 10¾ in., (27.3 cm.),
D. 8⅝ in., (21.9 cm.).
74.DE.27

27
ECUELLE
French; 1727.
Of silver-gilt. It is stamped with the Paris hallmark for 1727 and the mark of Claude-Gabriel Dardet (master 1715).
H. 4½ in., (11.4 cm.),
W. 11¾ in., (30 cm.),
D. 7⅛ in., (18.1 cm.).
71.DG.77

28
LONG-CASE CLOCK
French; c. 1725.
Veneered with brass and red painted tortoiseshell; set with bronze mounts, those at the corners of the clock representing the four continents. The movement is by J. F. Dominicé (active c. 1720). The maker of the case is not known.
H. 112 in., (284.5 cm.),
W. 27½ in., (70 cm.), D. 13 in., (33 cm.).
72.DA.40

29
PAIR OF LIDDED VASES
German (Meissen);
c. 1725–1730.
Each vase is marked beneath "AR" for Augustus Rex.
H. 14 in., (35.6 cm.), Diam. 8½ in., (21.6 cm.).
73.DE.65

30
TAPESTRY
French (Gobelins);
c. 1728–1730.
Woven for the Chancellor Chauvelin by Le Blond, after designs by Guy-Louis Vernasal and Claude Audran.
H. 133 in., (337.8 cm.), W. 104 in., (264.2 cm.).
65.DD.5

31
PAIR OF STANDING CANDELABRA (Girandoles)
(Illus. above cat. no. 19)
French; c. 1730.
Of gilt-bronze, set with drops of rock crystal.
H. 34 in., (86.3 cm.),
W. 24½ in., (62.3 cm.),
D. 14¾ in., (40 cm.).
75.DF.53

32
SET OF FOUR ARMCHAIRS
French; c. 1735.
Of gilded walnut, the maker unknown.
H. 42⅛ in., (104.5 cm.),
D. (at feet) 22 in., (55.9 cm.),
W. 25¾ in., (65.4 cm.).
75.DA.8

33
COMMODE
French; c. 1735.
Veneered with kingwood, set with gilt-bronze mounts, stamped "E. DOIRAT" (dates unknown).
H. 33¾ in., (85.9 cm.),
W. 66½ in., (168.9 cm.),
D. 28½ in., (72.4 cm.).
72.DA.66

34
PANELLED ROOM
French; c. 1735.
The room originally stood in the Hôtel Herlaut, on the Place Vendôme, Paris.
W. 264 in., (670.6 cm.),
L. 321½ in., (816.7 cm.),
H. 156 in., (396.2 cm.).
71.DH.118

35
PAIR OF FIREDOGS
(*Chenets*)
French; c. 1735.
Of gilded bronze.
H. 13½ in., (34.3 cm.),
W. 14 in., (35.5 cm.), D. 7 in.,
(17.8 cm.).
71.DF.114

36
DESK CHAIR
French; c. 1735.
The leather upholstery would appear to be original. There are lidded compartments lined with velvet in each arm. The maker is unknown.
H. 35⅞ in., (91 cm.),
W. 32¼ in., (81.9 cm.),
D. 26 in., (66 cm.).
71.DA.91

37
PAIR OF WALL LIGHTS
French; c. 1735.
Of gilt-bronze. The maker is unknown.
H. 22½ in., (57.2 cm.),
W. 11½ in., (29.2 cm.),
D. 15¾ in., (40 cm.).
J.P.G.J.11

38
PAIR OF FIREDOGS
(*Chenets*)
French; c. 1735.
Of gilt-bronze. The fire dogs are listed and described in the 1756 sale catalogue of Charles Cressent (1685–1768).
H. 15¼ in., (38.7 cm.),
W. 15 in., (38.1 cm.), D. 8 in., (20.3 cm.).
73.DF.63

39
WRITING DESK (*Bureau plat*)
French; c. 1735.
The table is veneered with tulipwood and set with gilt-bronze mounts. It is attributed to Charles Cressent (1685–1768).
H. 31¾ in., (80.7 cm.),
W. 76 in., (193 cm.), D. 39 in., (99.1 cm.).
55.DA.3

40
WALL CLOCK
French; c. 1735–1740.
Of gilt-bronze. The movement is by Jean-Jacques Fieffé (master 1725–1770), and the case is tentatively attributed to Charles Cressent (1685–1768).
H. 53 in., (134.6 cm.),
W. 24 in., (61 cm.), D. 6½ in., (16.5 cm.).
72.DB.89

41
COMMODE
French; c. 1735.
The commode is set with panels of red Japanese lacquer, decorated with gilt-bronze mounts. It is stamped "B.V.R.B." for Bernard van Risenburgh (master before 1730–1765/66).
H. 33¼ in., (84.5 cm.),
W. 45 in., (114.3 cm.),
D. 21¾ in., (55.2 cm.).
72.DA.46

42
FOLDING STOOL
French; c. 1735.
The gilt-wood folding stool is branded with the mark of the Château of Fontainebleau. The upholstery is modern.
H. 24 in., (61 cm), W. 26½ in., (67.3 cm.), D. 16¾ in., (42.5 cm.).
74.DA.46

43
COMMODE
French; c. 1737.
Set with a central panel of Japanese lacquer, the remaining areas painted with *vernis Martin,* a French imitation of oriental lacquer, and decorated with gilt-bronze mounts. The commode is stamped "B.V.R.B." for Bernard van Risenburgh (master before 1730–1765/66).
H. 35 in., (88.8 cm.),
W. 59¾ in., (151.9 cm.),
D. 21½ in., (54.6 cm.).
65.DA.4

44
PAIR OF CORNER CUPBOARDS (*Encoignures*)
French; c. 1740.
Set with panels of Japanese lacquer and veneered with ebony. Decorated with gilt-bronze mounts. Stamped "B.V.R.B." for Bernard van Risenburgh (master before 1730–1765/66).
H. 38¾ in., (98.4 cm.),
W. 33¾ in., (85.7 cm.),
D. 24¼ in., (61.6 cm.).
72.DA.44

45

SCREEN

French (Savonnerie); c. 1740.
The panels of carpet were knotted after designs by the animal painter Alexandre-François Desportes (1661–1743).
H. 71½ in., (181.6 cm.).
W. 96 in., (243.8 cm.).
75.DH.1

46
DOUBLE DESK
French; c. 1740
Veneered with tulipwood and kingwood, decorated with gilt-bronze mounts. The desk is stamped "B.V.R.B." for Bernard van Risenburgh (master before 1730–1765/66). Both sides of this double desk let down to form writing surfaces. The desk is reputed to have been bought in Paris in the 1760's by Lady Elizabeth Gunning.
H. 41¼ in., (104.8 cm.),
W. 60 in., (152.4 cm.),
D. 33 in., (83.8 cm.).
70.DA.87

47
SET OF FOUR
WALL LIGHTS
French; c. 1745.
The gilt-bronze wall lights are set with porcelain flowers.
H. 18 in., (45.7 cm.),
W. 13½ in., (34.3 cm.),
D. 7¾ in., (19.7 cm.).
75.DF.4

48
PAIR OF COMMODES
German (Munich); c. 1745.
Of gilded and painted pine. The decoration on the sides follows closely engravings by François de Cuvilliés (1698–1768), the architect to the King of Bavaria. The carving was probably executed by Joachim Dietrich (active 1736–1753).
H. 33 in., (83.8 cm.),
W. 54¾ in., (139.1 cm.),
D. 22½ in., (56.5 cm.).
72.DA.63

49
TABLE
The marble top: Italian (Roman); c. 1600.
The gilt-wood frame: French; c. 1745.
The white marble top is inlaid with colored marbles and semi-precious stones such as onyx and lapis lazuli.
H. 34½ in., (87.7 cm.),
W. 78 in., (198.1 cm.),
D. 45½ in., (115.6 cm.).
72.DA.58

50
COMMODE
French; c. 1745–1749.
Veneered with tulipwood and amaranth, and set with gilt-bronze mounts. The commode is described in the 1756 sale catalogue of Charles Cressent (1685–1768).
H. 35½ in., (90.2 cm.),
W. 53½ in., (135.9 cm.),
D. 25¼ in., (64.2 cm.).
70.DA.82

51
PLANISPHERE
(Astronomical clock)
French; c. 1745–1749.
Veneered with kingwood and set with bronze mounts. The movement (now missing) was made by Alexandre Fortier (dates unknown), and the case is attributed to Jean-Pierre Latz (c. 1691–1754). The clock once belonged to the Prince de Conti, and is listed in his sale catalogue of 1777.
H. 111 in., (281.9 cm.),
W. 37 in., (93.5 cm.),
D. 15 in., (38.1 cm.).
74.DB.2

52
WALL CLOCK
French; c. 1745–1749.
Of gilt-bronze. The movement is by Julien Le Roy (1686–1759, master 1713), and the case is by Jacques Caffieri (1678–1755, master 1714), whose signature appears below the dial.
H. 30½ in., (77.5 cm.),
W. 16 in., (40.6 cm.),
D. 4½ in., (11.4 cm.).
72.DA.45

53
PAIR OF LIDDED BOWLS
The ceramic: Chinese (Imari); c. 1740.
The gilt-bronze mounts: French; c. 1745–1749.
H. 12½ in., (31.8 cm.), Diam. 8½ in., (21.6 cm.).
72.DA.41

54
WRITING DESK *(Bureau plat)*
French; c. 1745–1749.
Veneered with tulipwood and ebony, decorated with gilt-bronze mounts. The table bears the stamp "B.V.R.B." for Bernard van Risenburgh (master before 1730–1765/66). The drawer fronts and the sides were probably once veneered with ebony or oriental lacquer.
H. 31 in., (78.7 cm.),
W. 63½ in., (161.3 cm.),
D. 32 in., (81.3 cm.).
J.P.G.D.13

55
WRITING DESK *(Bureau plat)*
French; c. 1745–1749.
Veneered with *satiné rouge*, decorated with gilt-bronze mounts. The table once belonged to Catherine II of Russia. The maker is unknown.
H. 31 in., (78.7 cm.),
W. 71⅜ in., (181.3 cm.),
D. 39¾ in., (101 cm.).
71.DA.95

56
TRAY
French; 1750.
The silver tray bears the Paris hallmark of 1750 and the stamp of François-Thomas Germain (master 1748–1791).
L. 8 7/16 in., (21.4 cm.), W. 7 7/16 in., (18.9 cm.).
71.DG.78

57
BOWL AND COVER
The gilt-bronze mounts: French; c. 1745–1749.
The porcelain: Chinese; c. 1740.
An inverted celadon bowl, slightly ground down in height, forms the lid to the identical bowl below.
H. 15¾ in., (40 cm.), Diam. 15 in., (38.1 cm.).
74.DE.19

58
PAIR OF STANDING CANDELABRA
The porcelain elephants: German (Meissen); c. 1741.
The gilt-bronze: French; c. 1750.
The elephants of Meissen porcelain were modelled by Peter Rienicke in 1741. The porcelain flowers are from the Vincennes manufactory which was established in 1745.
H. 9 in., (22.9 cm.), W. 9 in., (22.9 cm.), D. 4 in., (10.2 cm.).
75.DF.68

59

SET OF FOUR TAPESTRIES
French (Beauvais); c. 1750.
The tapestries show events from the story of Cupid and Psyche, and were woven after cartoons by François Boucher. The tapestry depicting "The Toilet of Psyche" is signed in the border "Besnier & Oudry à Beauvais," and both the "Abandonment of Psyche" and "Psyche at the Basketmakers" are signed "F. Boucher."
"The Arrival of Psyche at Cupid's Palace": H. 131 in., (332.7 cm.), W. 212 in., (538.5 cm.).
"The Toilet of Psyche:" H. 132 in., (335.3 cm.), W. 105 in., (266.7 cm.).
"The Abandonment of Psyche:" H. 143½ in., (364.5 cm.), W. 110 in., (279.4 cm.).
"Psyche at the Basketmakers:" H. 136 in., (345.5 cm.), W. 99 in., (251.5 cm.).
63.DD.2-5

60
INKSTAND
French; c. 1750.
The gilt-bronze inkstand is set with a panel of red Japanese lacquer, three mid-seventeenth century Chinese TeHua *blanc de chine* wine cups, and a group of three Chinese *blanc de chine* figures of the same date. The candle branch bears two lights.
H. 8 in., (20.3 cm.), W. 14 in., (35.6 cm.), D. 10½ in., (26.7 cm.).
76.DE.12

61
CLOCK AND BAROMETER
French; The barometer: c. 1735, The clock; c. 1750.
Of gilt-bronze. The cases of the clock and the barometer are attributed to Charles Cressent (1685–1768), and one of the brackets is signed "St. Germain" for Jean-Joseph de Saint-Germain (active in the second half of the eighteenth century). The face and movement of the clock are signed "Romilly à Paris," for Jean Romilly (1714–1796). The barometer is of nineteenth century date and replaces a clock movement.
Barometer: H. 34 in., (86.4 cm.), W. 15¼ in., (38.7 cm.), D. 6⅛ in., (15.6 cm.).
Clock: H. 34 in., (86.4 cm.), W. 15¾ in., (40 cm.), D. 6⅜ in., (16.2 cm.),
Brackets (of both): H. 16 in., (40.6 cm.), W. 17½ in., (44.5 cm.), D. 7¼ in., (18.4 cm.).

A PARIS

VARIABLE
TEMPETE
A PARIS

62

SET OF FOUR CORNER CUPBOARDS (*Encoignures*)

French; c. 1750.

The doors of the cupboards are set with marquetry panels of bunches of flowers in various stained woods—including rosewood, holly, and kingwood, set in a ground of lemonwood. The rest of the fronts are veneered with amaranth, and they are decorated with gilt-bronze mounts. The cupboards are attributed to Jean-Pierre Latz (c. 1691–1754). The marquetry is attributed to Jean-François Oeben (c. 1720, master 1761, died 1763).

A and B: H. 38 in., (96.5 cm.), W. 34 in., (86.4 cm.), D. 23¼ in., (59 cm.).

C and D: H. 35½ in., (90.2 cm.), W. 31 in., (78.7 cm.), D. 23 in., (58.4 cm.).

72.DA.39, 69.

63
PAIR OF COMMODES
French; c. 1750.
Veneered with tulipwood, kingwood, and amaranth; set with gilt-bronze mounts. The commodes are stamped "B.V.R.B." for Bernard van Risenburgh (master before 1730, died 1765/66). They once formed part of a set with four larger commodes and two corner cupboards reputedly made for the Hunting Lodge of the Elector of Saxony at Moritzburg. Two of the larger commodes now stand in the Museum fur Kunsthandwerk at Dresden, and the third remains at Moritzburg. The corner cupboards and a fourth commode were destroyed in the Second World War.
H. 34½ in., (87.6 cm.),
W. 34 in., (86.3 cm.),
D. 23½ in., (59.7 cm.).
71.DA.96

64
COMMODE
French; c. 1750.
Set with panels of Japanese lacquer, decorated with gilt-bronze mounts. The commode is attributed to Joseph Baumhauer (master 1767, d. 1772). Two trade labels of the *marchand mercier* Darnault are pasted above and below the piece.
H. 35¼ in., (87.6 cm.),
W. 57½ in., (146.1 cm.),
D. 24⅝ in., (62.6 cm.).
55.DA.2

65
VASE
The vase: Chinese; c. 1740.
The gilt-bronze mounts: French; c. 1750.
H. 14 in., (81.3 cm.), W. 16¾ in., (42.5 cm.), D. 11¼ in., (28.6 cm.).
72.DA.42

66
BOWL AND STAND
The bowl: Chinese; c. 1740.
The stand: Japanese (Imari); c. 1740.
The gilt-bronze mounts: French; c. 1750.
H. 7½ in., (19.1 cm.), Diam. 8 in., (20.3 cm.).
74.DE.28

67
MANTEL CLOCK
French; c. 1750.
Showing Europa and the bull, the clock is made of gilt-bronze, the bull patinated. The face and movement are signed "Étienne le Noir" (probably for Pierre-Étienne le Noir, born 1724, master 1743, date of death now known). The case is attributed to Robert Osmond (active second half of the eighteenth century).
H. 21½ in., (54.6 cm.), W. 17¾ in., (45.1 cm.), D. 9¼ in., (23.5 cm.).
73.DB.85

68

MECHANICAL TOILET AND WRITING TABLE

French; c. 1750.

Veneered with tulipwood, amaranth, *satiné rouge,* holly, and various stained exotic woods, decorated with gilt-bronze mounts. The table has mechanical fittings, enabling the top to slide back and a drawer in the frieze to emerge when the key is turned. The table is stamped beneath "J. F. OEBEN" for Jean-François Oeben (born c. 1720, royal cabinet-maker 1754, master 1761, died 1763).

H. 28¼ in., (71.7 cm.),
W. 29¼ in., (74.3 cm.),
D. 14¾ in., (37.5 cm.).
70.DA.84

69
TOILET AND
WRITING TABLE
French; c. 1754.
Veneered with burl ash, holly, tulipwood, and other stained and exotic woods; decorated with gilt-bronze mounts. The top slides back, and a frieze drawer is fitted with a sliding leather-covered lid which, when pushed back, reveals compartments lined with blue *moiré* silk. The table is stamped beneath "J. F. OEBEN" for Jean-François Oeben (born c. 1720, royal cabinet-maker 1754, master 1761, died 1763). An apparently identical table can be seen in a painting by Aved of Mme de Pompadour with her daughter Alexandrine, painted before 1754.
H. 28 in., (71.1 cm.),
W. 31½ in., (80 cm.),
D. 17 in., (43.2 cm.).
71.DA.103

70
COMMODE
French; c. 1755.
Veneered with tulipwood and kingwood, decorated with gilt-bronze mounts. The commode is stamped "DELORME" for Adrien-Faizelot Delorme (died after 1783) and "N. PETIT" for Nicolas Petit (born 1732, master 1761, died 1791). The commode was probably made by Delorme and sold in Petit's shop.
H. 35 in., (88.9 cm.),
W. 57½ in., (146.1 cm.),
D. 26½ in., (67.3 cm.).
70.DA.79

71
JARDINIERE
French (Vincennes); 1753.
The underside of the jardinière is painted with the date letter "A" for 1753, and an unknown painter's mark.
H. 8¾ in., (22.2 cm.),
W. 11¾ in., (30 cm.), D. 8¼ in., (21 cm.).
73.DE.64

72
WRITING TABLE
French; c. 1755.
Veneered with tulipwood and kingwood, set with gilt-bronze mounts. The table is stamped "B.V.R.B." for Bernard van Risenburgh (master before 1730, died 1765/66). A writing slide pulls out from the front, and slides to bear candlesticks pull out at the sides.
H. 29½ in., (75 cm.), W. 38 in., (96.5 cm.), D. 21½ in., (54.6 cm.).
65.DA.1

73
PAIR OF CORNER CUPBOARDS (*Encoignures*)
French; c. 1755.
Veneered with panels of Japanese lacquer, set with gilt-bronze mounts. Each cupboard is stamped "I. DUBOIS" for Jacques Dubois (born c. 1693, master 1742, died 1763).
H. 38½ in., (97.8 cm.),
W. 31 in., (78.7 cm.),
D. 23½ in., (59.7 cm.).
F.A.C.D.47, 48

74
VASE
The ceramic: Chinese; c. 1740.
The gilt-bronze mounts: French; c. 1755.
H. 14½ in., (36.9 cm.),
W. 5¼ in., (13.3 cm.), D. 5 in., (12.7 cm.).
75.DE.69

75
SECRETAIRE
French; c. 1755.
Veneered at the front with one large panel of red Japanese lacquer showing Europeans hunting, probably members of the Dutch East Indies Company. Decorated with gilt-bronze mounts. Stamped "I.DUBOIS" for Jacques Dubois (born c. 1693, master 1742, died 1763).
H. 40 in., (101.6 cm.),
W. 45½ in., (115.6 cm.),
D. 14¾ in., (37.5 cm.).
65.DA.3

76
TAPESTRY
French (Beauvais); between 1749 and 1772.
In 1749, François Boucher (1703–1770) designed a series of nine cartoons for a set of tapestries known as "The Loves of the Gods." Here, two cartoons have been joined together and woven as one tapestry. To the left is shown Bacchus and Ariadne, and to the right Antiope is surprised by Jupiter disguised as a satyr.
H. 144 in., (365.8 cm.),
W. 297 in., (754.4 cm.).
63.DD.6

77
PANELLED ROOM
French; c. 1755.
The panels made of carved, painted and gilded oak, with painted overdoors—formerly stood in an *hôtel* owned by Duc de Gramont on the Left Bank in Paris. It was moved to a new building on the Avenue Georges Mandel in 1910. That house was demolished in 1969. The ceiling is an exact copy of the original.
H. 192 in., (487.7 cm.),
W. 282½ in., (717.6 cm.),
D. 306 in., (777.2 cm.).
73.DH.107

78
PLATEAU
French (Sèvres); c. 1758.
Decorated with a ground of rose Pompadour. Marked on its undersurface with the crossed L's of the Sèvres manufactory, the date letter "F" for 1758, and an unidentified painter's mark.
W. 5 in., (12.7 cm.), D. 5 in., (12.7 cm.), H. ⅞ in., (2.2 cm.).
72.DE.75

79
PAIR OF CUPS AND SAUCERS
French (Sèvres); 1759.
Decorated with a ground of rose Pompadour and apple green. The saucers painted on their undersurfaces with the crossed L's of the Sèvres manufactory, together with the date letter "G" for 1759 and the painter's mark for Charles Buteux.
H. (Cup): 3⅜ in., (8.6 cm.), Diam., 3⅛ in., (7.9 cm.).
H. (Saucer): 1⅝ in., (4.1 cm.), Diam. 6⅛ in., (15.6 cm.).
72.DE.74

80
PAIR OF STANDING CANDELABRA
(Vases à flambeaux)
French (Sèvres); c. 1759.
Decorated with rose Pompadour and apple green, with gilding. One bears the crossed L's of the Sèvres manufactory, the date letter "G" for 1759, and the letter "K" for the painter Dodin. Only two other pairs of this model are known to exist today, and one may be seen at the Metropolitan Museum of Art, New York.
H. 9¾ in., (24.8 cm.), W. 6 in., (15.2 cm.), D. 3½ in., (8.9 cm.).
75.DE.65

81
WRITING TABLE
French; c. 1760.
Veneered with green stained burl ash and amaranth, decorated with gilt-bronze mounts. At the front, a small writing slide may be pulled out beneath the top, and a drawer at the side is fitted with silvered compartments that originally held ink and sand pots and a sponge box. The table is stamped twice inside the lower front drawer "DELORME" for Adrien Delorme (master 1748).
H. 27 in., (68.6 cm.),
W. 11¾ in., (29.8 cm.),
D. 9⅝ in., (24.5 cm.).
72.DA.64

82
TOILET TABLE
French; c. 1760.
Veneered with tulipwood, amaranth, sycamore maple, holly, and other stained and exotic woods. The frieze drawer contains a lid and a hinged mirror, and one of the deep lidded side drawers is fitted for cosmetic pots. The table is not stamped with a maker's name, but it is attributed to Jean-François Leleu (born 1729, master 1764, died 1807).
H. 27¾ in., (70.5 cm.),
W. 22½ in., (57.2 cm.),
D. 15½ in., (39.4 cm.).
72.DA.49

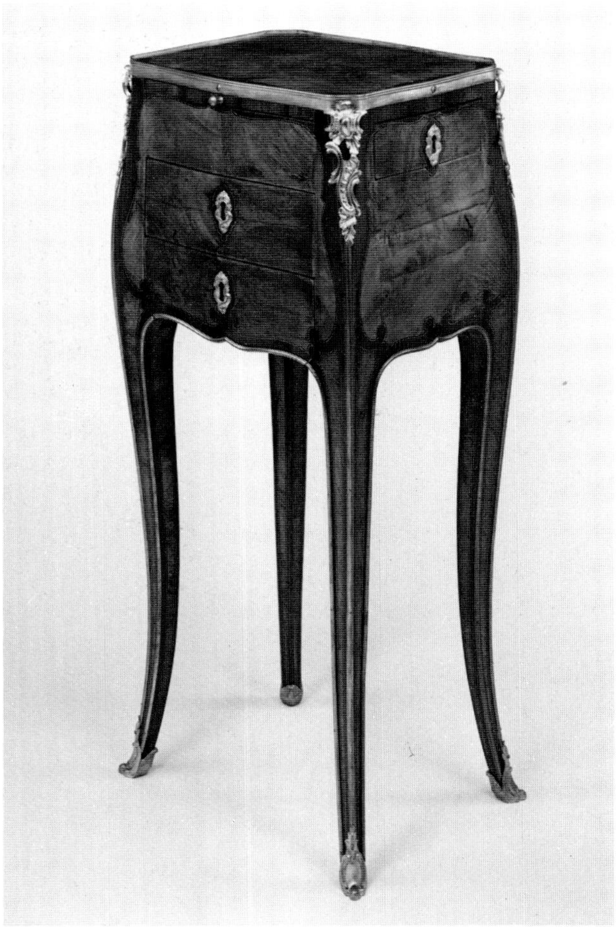

83
COMMODE
French; c. 1760.
Veneered with tulipwood and kingwood, decorated with gilt-bronze mounts. The commode is stamped beneath the marble top "J. F. OEBEN" for Jean-François Oeben (born c. 1720, royal cabinet-maker 1754, master 1761, died 1763).
H. 36 in., (91.4 cm.),
W. 54½ in., (138.5 cm.),
D. 18¼ in., (46.3 cm.).
72.DA.54

84
CARD TABLE
French; c. 1760.
Veneered with tulipwood, kingwood, and green stained burl wood; decorated with gilt-bronze feet. The top may be pulled forward, then opened up to provide a baize-covered surface for playing cards. The table is stamped beneath "J. F. OEBEN" for Jean-François Oeben (born c. 1720, royal cabinet-maker 1754, master 1761, died 1763).
H. 27¾ in., (70.5 cm.),
W. 33½ in., (85.1 cm.),
D. 14½ in., (36.9 cm.).
71.DA.105

85
WALL CLOCK
AND BRACKET
French; c. 1760.
Made of gilt-bronze; veneered with panels of red, green, and cream painted horn. The movement is signed "Lapina" (dates unknown), the case and bracket are stamped "ANT. FOVLLET" for Antoine Foullet (born 1710, master 1749, died 1775).
H. 46¾ in., (118.7 cm.),
W. 19½ in., (49.5 cm.),
D. 11¼ in., (28.6 cm.).
75.DB.7

86
JARDINIERE
French; c. 1760.
Gilt-bronze, set with Sèvres plaques. The back is removable, as is an interior tin compartment made to hold flowers or bulbs. A Sèrves jardinière at the Metropolitan Museum of Art, New York is painted with an identical scene, known as "The Marriage Contract," and it is dated for 1760, and bears the letter "K" for the painter Dodin.
H. 6½ in., (16.5 cm.),
W. 11½ in., (29.2 cm.),
D. 5½ in., (14 cm.).
73.DE.62

87
POT POURRI VASE
(Vaisseau à mât)
French (Sèvres); c. 1761.
Decorated with rose Pompadour and apple green, with gilding. Only thirteen of these vases are thought to have been made at the Sèvres manufactory, and ten are known to exist today.
H. 15 in., (38.1 cm.),
W. 13¾ in., (35 cm.),
D. 6¾ in., (17.2 cm.).
75.DE.11

88
TABLE
French; c. 1761.
The frame is lacquered with green, blue and gold *vernis Martin,* and the top is set with a tray of Sèvres porcelain. The underside of the drawer is stamped "B.V.R.B." for Bernard van Risenburgh (master before 1730, died 1765/66), and the tray is painted beneath with the crossed L's of the Sèvres manufactory, the date letter "I" for 1761, and the letter "K" for the painter Dodin.
H. 26½ in., (67.4 cm.),
W. 12¾ in., (32.4 cm.),
D. 10½ in., (26.7 cm.).
70.DA.85

89
JARDINIERE
(*Cuvette Mahon*)
French (Sèvres); 1761.
Decorated with rose Pompadour, with blue trellis work at the front, *oeil-de-perdrix* at the sides, and *vermiculé* on the back. The scene on the front is taken from a detail of a Teniers painting—now at the Hermitage Museum, Leningrad—of a village fête. The jardinière bears the crossed L's for the Sèvres manufactory, the date letter "I" for 1761, and the letter "M," which was probably used by the painter Morin.
H. 6¼ in., (15.9 cm.), W. 9 in., (22.9 cm.), D. 4¾ in., (12.1 cm.).
72.DE.65

90
SAUCE BOAT
French; 1762.
Of silver; the interior of the boat is silver-gilt. It is stamped with the Paris hallmark for 1762 and with the mark of Jean-Baptiste Cheret (master 1759, died 1788).
H. 4 5/16 in., (11 cm.),
W. 7 9/16 in., (19.2 cm.),
D. 5⅝ in., (14.3 cm.).
71.DG.76

91
CABINET
French; c. 1765
Veneered with *bois-de-rose,* amaranth, and green stained wood; set with gilt-bronze mounts. The two tambour doors enclose a marble based compartment above, and three drawers below. A drawer in the side of the frieze contains gilt-bronze boxes that originally held an ink pot, sand pot, and sponge box. The interior of the drawer is stamped "R.V.L.C." for Roger Vandercruse LaCroix (master 1755, died after 1780).
H. 37 in., (93.9 cm.),
W. 23½ in., (59.7 cm.),
D. 17½ in., (44.5 cm.).
70.DA.81

92
PAIR OF CHAIRS
French; c. 1765.
The frames are of gilded beechwood, the silk velvet upholstery is modern. Both chairs are branded with the mark of the Château of Versailles, and stamped "J. BOUCAULT" for Jean Boucault (born c. 1705, master 1728, died 1786). Another identical chair, also branded with the Versailles mark, is in the William Rockhill Nelson Gallery of Art, Kansas City. Four chairs were once *en suite* with two armchairs and a settee.
H. 35½ in., (90.1 cm.),
W. 23½ in., (59.7 cm.),
D. 26 in., (66.1 cm.).
71.DA.92

93
TOILET AND WRITING TABLE
French; c. 1765.
Veneered with various stained woods and tulipwood, set with gilt-bronze mounts. Both the top and the frieze are decorated with panels of "naive" marquetry, showing ruins and peopled landscapes. Once brightly colored, now only the green stained wood retains its unfaded pigment. The top slides back, and the frieze drawer is fitted with two lidded compartments centered by a hinged velvet-covered book rest. The table is not stamped with a maker's name, but it is attributed to Louis-Noël Malle (born 1734, master 1765, died 1782). An almost identical table is in the California Palace of the Legion of Honor, San Francisco.
H. 28¼ in., (71.7 cm.),
W. 32⅝ in., (82.9 cm.),
D. 17⅛ in., (43.5 cm.).
72.DA.67

94
MANTEL CLOCK
French; c. 1765.
Of gilt-bronze, the female figures represent sidereal and terrestrial time. The movement is by Charles le Roy (born 1709, master 1733, died 1771); the maker of the case is unknown.
H. 28 in., (71.1 cm.),
W. 23½ in., (59.7 cm.),
D. 12¾ in., (32.4 cm.).
73.DB.78

95
COMMODE
French; 1769.
Veneered with tulipwood, holly, and ebony; decorated with gilt-bronze mounts. The commode, with a companion piece that is now missing, was delivered to the Château of Versailles on the 28th August, 1769 for the bed chamber of Madame Louise, one of the daughters of Louis XV. It was made by the royal cabinet-maker Gilles Joubert (born 1689, royal cabinet-maker 1763–1774, died 1775).
H. 36½ in., (92.7 cm.), W. 71 in., (180.3 cm.), D. 27 in., (68.6 cm.).
55.DA.5

96
MUSIC STAND
French; c. 1770.
Veneered with tulipwood and pearwood, incised with colored mastic, set with gilt-bronze mounts. The music rest swivels and can be lowered and raised. The column of the stand can also be raised and lowered by means of a ratchet. The arms supporting the candle sockets are adjustable. The stand is not stamped with the maker's name, but it is attributed to Martin Carlin (master 1766, died 1785).
H. 47½ in., (120.6 cm.), W. 20 in., (50.8 cm.), D. 14½ in., (36.8 cm.).
55.DA.4

97
TABLE
French; c. 1770.
Veneered with tulipwood, ebony, and holly; set with Sèvres porcelain plaques; and decorated with gilt-bronze mounts. The lower shelf is surfaced with white marble. The circular plaque which forms the top of the table bears on its undersurface the crossed L's of the Sèvres manufactory, and the date letter "L" for 1765. There is no painter's mark. The table is not stamped, but it is attributed to Martin Carlin (master 1766, died 1785).
H. 27⅝ in., (70.2 cm.), Diam. 15¼ in., (38.7 cm.).
70.DA.74

98
TABLE
French; c. 1773.
Veneered with tulipwood, ebony, and holly; set with Sèvres plaques; and decorated with gilt-bronze mounts. The circular plaque which forms the top of the table is marked beneath with the crossed L's of the Sèvres manufactory, the date 1773, and a cross which is probably the mark of the painter, Mlle. Xhrouet. The table is stamped "M. CARLIN" for Martin Carlin (master 1766, died 1785).
H. 28¾ in., (73 cm.), Diam. 16¼ in., (41.2 cm.).
70.DA.75

99
SET OF SIX PAINTED
SILK PANELS
French; c. 1771.
The silk satin is painted with gouache, heightened with gold. The first panel bears the monograms "MJL" and "LSX" which must be for Maria Josephine Louise and Louis Stanislas Xavier, who were married on May 4, 1771. Louis became Louis XVIII in 1814. Two more panels from this set are in the Musée des Arts Décoratifs, Paris.
H. 57 in., (144.8 cm.),
W. 7 in., (17.8 cm.).
73.DH.89

100
SECRETAIRE
French; c. 1775.
Veneered with tulipwood and boxwood, incised with colored mastics, set with Sèvres plaques, and decorated with gilt-bronze mounts. The fall front forms a writing surface and reveals small drawers and pigeon holes. The central round Sèvres plaque bears on its back the crossed L's for the Sèvres manufactory, the date letter "X" for 1775, and the mark for the flower painter Pierre *le jeune* (active 1763–1800). The secrétaire is stamped "M. CARLIN" for Martin Carlin (master 1766, died 1785).
H. 46¾ in., (118.7 cm.),
W. 36 in., (91.4 cm.),
D. 13 in., (33 cm.).
65.DA.2

101
SECRETAIRE
French; c. 1775.
Veneered with kingwood, tulipwood, and lemonwood; incised with red mastic; and set with studs of mother-of-pearl. Decorated with gilt-bronze mounts. The fall front lets down to form a writing surface and reveals small drawers and pigeon holes. The secrétaire is stamped "I. DUBOIS" for René Dubois (born 1737, master 1754, died 1799), who used the same stamp as his father, Jacques Dubois.
H. 62¾ in., (159.4 cm.),
W. 27¼ in., (69.2 cm.),
D. 13¼ in., (33.7 cm.).
72.DA.60

102
VASE
French; c. 1775.
Of Egyptian porphyry, mounted with gilt-bronze.
H. 16 in., (40.6 cm.), W. 16½ in., (41.9 cm.), D. 9½ in., (24.1 cm.).
73.DH.88

103
PAIR OF STANDING CANDELABRA
French; c. 1775.
Of gilt-bronze. They are fitted with gilt-bronze stoppers, formed of clusters of fruit and flowers, which can be put in the candle sockets in place of candles. They are attributed to Pierre Gouthière (born 1732, master 1758, died 1813/14).
H. 16 in., (40.6 cm.), W. 9 in., (22.9 cm.), D. 9 in., (22.9 cm.).
72.DA.43

104
SET OF FOUR WALL LIGHTS
French; c. 1775.
Of gilt-bronze. These wall lights may once have belonged to the Prince de Condé as identical lights appear in a watercolor dating to about 1784 of the salon at Chantilly.
H. 27 in., (68.6 cm.), W. 13¼ in., (33.7 cm.), D. 10½ in., (26.7 cm.).
74.DF.3, 1948, 12–13, 16–17

105
SECRETAIRE
French; c. 1776.
Veneered with tulipwood and amaranth, set with Sèvres porcelain plaques, and decorated with gilt-bronze mounts. The four Sèvres plaques are all marked with the crossed L's of the Sèvres manufactory, and the date letter "Y" for 1776, and two of them bear the symbol for the flower painter Jean-Baptiste Tandart (act. 1754–1803). The underside of the upper part of the cabinet is inscribed in pencil "Saunier le Jeune 1776" and the cabinet is also stamped "C. C. SAUNIER" for Claude-Charles Saunier (born 1735, master 1752, died 1807). The stand for the cabinet is of early twentieth-century date and is stamped "F. DURAND FILS."
H. 50 in., (127 cm.),
W. 29½ in., (75 cm.),
D. 16¾ in., (42.6 cm.).
67.DA.7

106

TABLE

French; 1777.

Veneered with satinwood and amaranth, decorated with gilt-bronze mounts. The table was delivered to the Petit Trianon at Versailles on the 6th August, 1777 for use in the *cabinet* of Louis XVI. It was ordered by Marie Antoinette, and was made by the royal cabinet-maker Jean-Henri Riesener (born 1734, master 1768, royal cabinet-maker 1774 to 1784, died 1806). The surface was originally covered with black velvet, bordered with silver braid. A secrétaire and a small table, delivered to the Trianon by Riesener on the same day, are now in the James A. de Rothschild Collection at Waddesdon Manor, England. A commode, also delivered at the same time, is now in a private collection in Paris.

H. 28½ in., (72.4 cm.),
W. 53½ in., (135.9 cm.),
D. 28 in., (71.1 cm.).
71.DA.102

107
PAIR OF *FAMILLE ROSE*
LIDDED VASES
Chinese (Ch'ien Lung period); 1736–1795.
H. 24¼ in., (61.6 cm.), Diam. 13¼ in., (33.7 cm.).
72.DE.62

108
SET OF FOUR CHAIRS
French; c. 1780.
The frames are of gilded beechwood, the silk upholstery is modern. One of the chairs bears the stencil of the *Garde Meuble de la Reine* beneath the frame, showing that the set was originally ordered for Marie Antoinette. An armchair, in a private collection in Paris which is part of this set is stamped "G. JACOB" for Georges Jacob (born 1739, master 1765, died 1814). It also bears the mark of the Château Trianon. This set of four chairs may therefore be attributed to Georges Jacob.
H. 35 in., (88.9 cm.), W. 21 in., (53.3 cm.), D. 20 in., (50.8 cm.).
71.DA.93

109
SET OF FOUR TAPESTRIES
French (Gobelins);
c. 1776–1778.
The four tapestries, woven at the Gobelins manufactory after cartoons by François Boucher (1703–1770), were given by Louis XVI to the Grand Duke Paul Petrovich (later Czar Paul I) and his wife Maria Feodorovna when they traveled through Paris in 1782. They were hung at the Palace of Pavlovsk near Leningrad.

"Venus and Vulcan:" François Boucher painted the picture from which the cartoon for this tapestry was made in 1764, and it now hangs in the Grand Trianon at Versailles.
H. 150 in., (381 cm.),
W. 192 in., (487.7 cm.).
71.DD.468

"Venus on the Waters:" François Boucher painted the cartoon for this tapestry between 1763 and 1764, and it was discovered at the Gobelins in 1870. It disappeared during the uprising of *La Commune* in 1871.
H. 151 in., (383.5 cm.),
W. 125 in., (317.5 cm.).
71.DD.467

"Aurora and Cephalus:" François Boucher painted the picture from which the cartoon for this tapestry was made in 1764. It now hangs in the Musée du Louvre, Paris.
H. 150 in., (381 cm.),
W. 127 in., (322.5 cm.).
71.DD.469

"Diana and Callisto and Vertumnus and Pomona:" The painting for the cartoon of this tapestry, by François Boucher, is dated 1769. It now hangs in the Wallace Collection, London.
H. 151 in., (383.5 cm.),
W. 246 in., (624.8 cm.).
71.DD.466

110
PANELLED ROOM
French; c. 1780
Of painted oak. The floor and the mantelpiece, though of eighteenth-century date, are not original to the room. The cast iron fireback and the windows are modern, while the plaster cornice and ceiling rosette are modern copies of eighteenth-century originals. Unfortunately the origins of this fairly simple room are not known.
W. 257 in., (652.8 cm.),
D. 366 in., (929.6 cm.).
61.DH.1

111
PAIR OF CANDLESTICKS
French; c. 1780.
Of gilt-bronze. Each is signed beneath "MARTINCOURT" for Etienne Martincourt (active in the second half of the eighteenth century) who was one of the few *bronziers* to sign his works.
H. 11⅞ in., (30.2 cm.), Diam. (at base) 5¼ in., (13.3 cm.).
72.DF.48

112
PAIR OF URNS
French; c. 1780.
Of Egyptian porphyry, mounted with gilt-bronze. An identical pair of urns, now in the Musée du Louvre, were bought by Louis XVI at the sale of the Duc d'Aumont in 1782. They were probably made at the *Menus Plaisirs* after designs by Belanger, the mounts made by Pierre Gouthière (born 1732, master 1758, died 1813/14).
H. 14 in., (35.6 cm.), Diam. 9 in., (22.9 cm.).
74.DH.24

113
STANDING VASE
The porcelain: Chinese; c. 1750.
The mounts: French; c. 1780.
The blue vase is of Chinese porcelain, and the mounts of gilt-bronze. It was reputedly bought at the Revolutionary sales of Versailles by the Polish Countess Isabella Lubomirska (1736–1816), a friend of Marie Antoinette. The vase was acquired by the Museum from her great-grandson, Count Potocki. The pair to it is in the British Royal Collections at Windsor Castle. It was bought by George IV (then Prince Regent), from Thomire et Cie in Paris in 1814. It is probable that the second vase was also bought at the sale of Versailles by the famous *bronzier* Thomire, who was a colleague of Pierre Gouthière. The gilt-bronze mounts on the vase are attributed to the latter's hand.
H. 31½ in., (80 cm.), Diam. 22½ in., (57.2 cm.).
70.DE.115

114
PAIR OF FIREDOGS
French; c. 1780.
Of gilt-bronze, these firedogs are described in some detail in the 1781 sale catalogue of the Duchess de Mazarin, where they are stated to be "par Goutière." Documented works by the *bronzier* Pierre Gouthière (born 1732, master 1758, died 1813/14) are extremely rare.
H. 15¾ in., (40 cm.), W. 15 in., (38.1 cm.), D. 5½ in., (14 cm.).
62.DF.1

115
PAIR OF WALL LIGHTS
French; c. 1781.
Of gilt-bronze. An identical pair of wall lights were made by Pierre Gouthière (born 1732, master 1758, died 1813/14) for the Duchess de Mazarin in 1781, after models in wax made by the architect François-Joseph Belanger (born 1744, appointed *dessinateur des Menus Plaisirs* in 1767, died 1818). These wall lights may therefore be given to the hand of Gouthière.
H. 20½ in., (52.1 cm.),
W. 11¾ in., (29.8 cm.),
D. 7 in., (17.8 cm.).
74.DF.5

116
PAIR OF STANDING CANDELABRA
French; c. 1784.
Of gilt-bronze, with blued metal bodies and drip pans. The candelabra may have formed part of a set of objects delivered to Mesdames at the Château of Bellevue in 1784 by L. F. Feuchères (born c. 1760, died 1828). A set of four wall lights, also probably part of the set, are at the Philadelphia Museum of Art, while the Museé du Louvre possesses a pair of celadon vases from Bellevue bearing the same gilt-bronze mounts.
H. 44¾ in., (113.7 cm.),
W. 17¾ in., (45.1 cm.),
D. 10½ in., (26.7 cm.).
71.DF.99

117
SECRETAIRE
French; c. 1780.
Veneered with amboyna wood, set with Sèvres porcelain plaques, and decorated with gilt-bronze mounts. The fall front lets down to form a writing surface, revealing small drawers and pigeon holes. One of the oval porcelain plaques is marked with the crossed L's of the Sèvres manufactory and the number 2000, all in gold. The number is the mark for the gilder Vincent *le jeune* (active 1753–1806). The secrétaire is not stamped with a maker's name, but it is attributed to Adam Weisweiler (born 1750, master 1778, died after 1810).
H. 47½ in., (120.6 cm.),
W. 32 in., (81.3 cm.),
D. 14¾ in., (37.5 cm.).
70.DA.83

118
BONHEUR-DU-JOUR
French; c. 1785.
Veneered with amboyna wood, set with gilt-bronze mounts, and decorated with Wedgwood plaques. The desk is not stamped with a maker's name, but it is attributed to Adam Weisweiler (born c. 1750, master 1778, died after 1810).
the Wedgwood plaques were designed by Lady Templeton, and were first modeled by Hackwood in 1783.
H. 42½ in., (108 cm.),
W. 27¼ in., (69.2 cm.),
D. 16¼ in., (41.2 cm.).
72.DA.59

119
ROLL-TOP DESK
German; c. 1785.
Veneered with Cuban mahogany, decorated with gilt-bronze mounts. The desk is not stamped with a maker's name, but it is attributed to David Roentgen (born 1743, master 1780, died 1807). The gilt-bronze mounts are probably of German make, with the exception of the gilt-bronze plaque above the roll-top, which is attributed to Pierre Gouthière (born 1732, master 1758, died 1813/14). The desk is fitted with elaborate mechanical devices.
H. 65 in., (165.1 cm.),
W. 59⅛ in., (150.3 cm.),
D. 33½ in., (85.1 cm.).
72.DA.47

120
SECRETAIRE
French; c. 1785.
Veneered with panels of Japanese lacquer and ebony, decorated with gilt-bronze mounts. The fall front lets down to form a writing surface and reveals small drawers and pigeon holes. The desk is not stamped with a maker's name, but it is attributed to Jean-Henri Riesener (born 1734, master 1768, royal cabinet-maker 1774–1784, died 1801). The gilt-bronze plaque on the fall front, known as "The Sacrifice to Cupid," was probably copied after a relief by Clodion (1738–1814).
H. 60¾ in., (154.3 cm.),
W. 44¾ in., (113.7 cm.),
D. 18¼ in., (46.3 cm.).
71.DA.104

121
ROLL-TOP DESK
French; c. 1785.
Veneered with mahogany, decorated with gilt-bronze mounts. The interior is fitted with four small drawers with four large pigeon holes above them. The large drawer to the left of the kneehole is fitted with a strong-box, and writing slides pull out from the sides of the desk. One of the small interior drawers is stamped "B. MOLITOR" for Bernard Molitor (born 1730, master 1787, died after 1811).
H. 53½ in., (153.9 cm.),
W. 70 in., (177.8 cm.),
D. 33 in., (83.8 cm.).
67.DA.9

122
PAIR OF CABINETS
A: French; c. 1785.
B: French; c. 1810.
Veneered with ebony, set with pewter stringing, decorated with *pietre dure* plaques, and mounted with gilt-bronze. The late eighteenth-century cabinet is set with seventeenth-century *pietre dure* plaques that were probably made by Italian craftsmen working at the Gobelins workshops. It is attributed to Adam Weisweiler (born c. 1750, master 1778, died after 1810). This cabinet appeared in two Paris sales of the 1790's, and it is probable that it was bought by the famous English dilettante William Beckford. It is likely that he ordered the pair to be made, perhaps in the post revolutionary workshops of Adam Weisweiler. It is mounted with *pietre dure* plaques of early seventeenth, late seventeenth, and late eighteenth-century date. The small roundels are of mosaic and date from the early years of the nineteenth-century. They were made in Rome.
H. 39¾ in., (101 cm.),
W. 59¼ in., (150.6 cm.),
D. 20¾ in., (52.7 cm.).
76.DA.9

123
PAIR OF LIDDED BOWLS
French; c. 1785.
The bowls and lids are of Sèvres *bleu-du-roi* porcelain, mounted with gilt-bronze. They were used to hold pot-pourri.
H. 14¾ in., (37.5 cm.), Diam. 14½ in., (36.9 cm.).
73.DE.77

124
PAIR OF STANDING TAZZAS
French; c. 1785.
The marble bowls are mounted with gilt-bronze and stand on yellow Sienna marble plinths. They were probably used to contain burning incense.
H. 15 in., (38.1 cm.),
W. 10¾ in., (27.3 cm.),
D. 10¾ in., (27.3 cm.).
74.DF.4

125
CHAIR
French; c. 1787.
Of carved beech, with a caned seat and back. The velvet upholstery is modern. This *chaise à toilette* forms part of a set delivered by Georges Jacob (born 1739, master 1765, died 1814) to Marie Antoinette's *chambre à coucher du Treillage* in 1787. The set originally consisted of two armchairs, two side chairs, a firescreen, a stool, and a bed. With the exception of the bed, the rest of the set has now been returned to the Petit Trianon at Versailles. Originally, this chair was painted in natural colors, now stripped.
H. 33½ in., (85.1 cm.),
W. 22¾ in., (57.8 cm.),
D. 21½ in., (54.6 cm.).
72.DA.51

126
PAIR OF FOLDING STOOLS
French; c. 1786.
Of carved beech; painted white, and gilded. The upholstery is modern. The stools once formed part of a set of sixty-four which were delivered to the Gaming Rooms of Marie Antoinette at the Châteaux of Fontainebleau and Compiègne in 1786 and 1787. They were made by Jean-Baptiste-Claude Sené (born 1748, master 1769, died 1803). They were carved by Vallois, and the original gilding was by Chatard and Chaudron. Twenty-four of these stools have now been returned to the Château of Fontainebleau.
W. 28 in., (71.1 cm.),
D. 19¼ in., (48.9 cm.),
H. 17 in., (43.2 cm.).
71.DA.94

127
CABINET
French; c. 1785–1790.
Veneered with ebony, set with a panel of late seventeenth-century "boulle" marquetry made of pewter, brass, and tortoiseshell at the front, and set at the sides with panels of similar date composed of pewter, rosewood, and ebony. Decorated with gilt-bronze mounts, the figures of Summer and Autumn and the masks at the sides are of late seventeenth-century or early eighteenth-century date. The cabinet is not stamped with a maker's name, but it is attributed to Philippe-Claude Montigny (born 1734, master 1766, died 1800).
H. 41½ in., (105.4 cm.),
W. 64½ in., (163.9 cm.),
D. 22 in., (55.9 cm.).
72.DA.71

128
BRONZE GROUP
French; c. 1785–1790.
The group shows Hebe rejuvenating Aeson, the father of Jason. It is attributed to the hand of the sculptor Louis-Simon Boizot (born 1743, elected to the Academie of Saint Luc in 1778, died 1809). Boizot also provided models for furniture mounts.
H. 26½ in., (67.4 cm.),
W. 22½ in., (57.2 cm.),
D. 14 in., (35.6 cm.).
74.PB.6

129
MANTEL CLOCK
(*Pendule squelette*)
French; c. 1790–1800.
Of gilt-bronze with enameled plaques, standing on a white marble base, and covered with a glass case. The dial is signed "Folin l'ainé A PARIS" for Nicolas-Alexandre Folin (master 1784), and the enamel is signed "G. Merlet" for an enameller who was active in the late eighteenth and early nineteenth centuries.
H. 19⅜ in., (49.2 cm.),
W. 10¾ in., (27.3 cm.),
D. 2½ in., (6.4 cm.).
72.DB.57

Folin l'Ainé
A PARIS

130
ELEPHANT
Chinese (Ch'ien Lung period); 1736–1795.
Porcelain. The elephant was produced rather early in the period, and was made for the export market.
H. 22½ in., (57.2 cm.),
W. 10 in., (25.4 cm.), D. 13 in., (33 cm.).
72.DE.61

131
PAIR OF ICE VASES
(*Seaux à Bouteilles*)
French (Sèvres); 1792.
Of porcelain, painted black, decorated with two tones of gold and platinum. The vases are marked with the crossed L's of the Sèvres manufactory, with the date letters "OO" for 1792 and the symbol for the painter Dieux.
H. 6½ in., (16.5 cm.),
W. 9½ in., (23.5 cm.),
D. 7¼ in., (18.4 cm.).
72.DE.53.

132
SET OF SEAT FURNITURE
French; c. 1810.
Of mahogany, decorated with gilt-bronze mounts, upholstered with Beauvais tapestry. The set consists of a settee, eight armchairs, and two *bergères*. It formerly belonged to Eugene Beauharnais, the brother of Josephine, and, by 1814, to Czar Alexander I. The pieces are not stamped with a maker's name, but they were probably made at the workshops of Jacob Desmalter et Cie, a company run by the two sons of the famous chairmaker Georges Jacob.
Settee: H. 39¾ in., (101 cm.), W. 74½ in., (189.3 cm.), D. 24½ in., (61.6 cm.).
Bergères: H. 39¾ in., (101 cm.), W. 25¾ in., (65.5 cm.), D. 19¼ in., (48.9 cm.).
Armchairs: H. 39¾ in., (101 cm.), W. 25 in., (63.5 cm.), D. 19¼ in., (48.9 cm.).
67.DA.6

133
INKSTAND
French; c. 1810.
Of white marble, set with gilt-bronze mounts, backed by velvet. The maker is unknown.
H. 3½ in., (8.9 cm.), W. 18½ in., (47 cm.), D. 9½ in., (24.1 cm.).
73.DH.67

134
CHANDELIER
French; c. 1810.
Of gilt-bronze, with a blue enameled metal globe, set with glass drops. The chandelier is in the shape of an air balloon. The first of these balloons was released from the grounds of Versailles in 1783 by Montgolfier brothers, and quickly began a vogue for balloon-shaped objects. The maker of the chandelier is not known.
H. 51 in., (129.5 cm.), Diam. 38 in., (96.5 cm.).
73.DH.76

135
SECRETAIRE
French; c. 1824.
Veneered with amaranth, set with porcelain plaques, and decorated with gilt-bronze mounts. The fall front lets down to form a writing surface, revealing drawers and pigeon holes which are veneered with thuya wood, ebony, and pewter. The secrétaire is not stamped with a maker's name but it is attributed to Alexandre-Louis Bellangé (born 1799, died after 1874).
H. 61 in., (154.9 cm.),
W. 34 in., (86.3 cm.),
D. 16½ in., (41.9 cm.).
66.DA.1

MUSEUM PUBLICATIONS

Guidebooks
The J. Paul Getty Museum Guidebook
Herculaneum to Malibu: A Companion to the Guidebook

Catalogues
Catalogue of the Ancient Art
Catalogue of the Paintings
The J. Paul Getty Museum

Journals
The J. Paul Getty Museum Journal I
The J. Paul Getty Museum Journal II
The J. Paul Getty Museum Journal III

The J. Paul Getty Museum Series
Benvenuto di Giovanni and Girolamo di Benvenuto
The Statue of Cybele
The Cassone Paintings of Francesco di Giorgio
The Collaboration of Niccoló Tegliacci and Luca di Tommé
Giovanni di Francesco and the Master of Pratovecchio
The Artists of the Mummy Portraits
The Terracottas of the Tarantine Greeks

Museum Publications
Alma Tadema's *Spring*
The Ardabil Carpets
The Bronze Statue of a Youth
French 18th-Century Clocks in the J. Paul Getty Museum
The Conservation of Ancient Marble
The Herb in Antiquity
A Greek Prayer

For additional titles and information, contact:
Publications Department
The J. Paul Getty Museum
17985 Pacific Coast Highway
Malibu, California 90265